Telling Trails

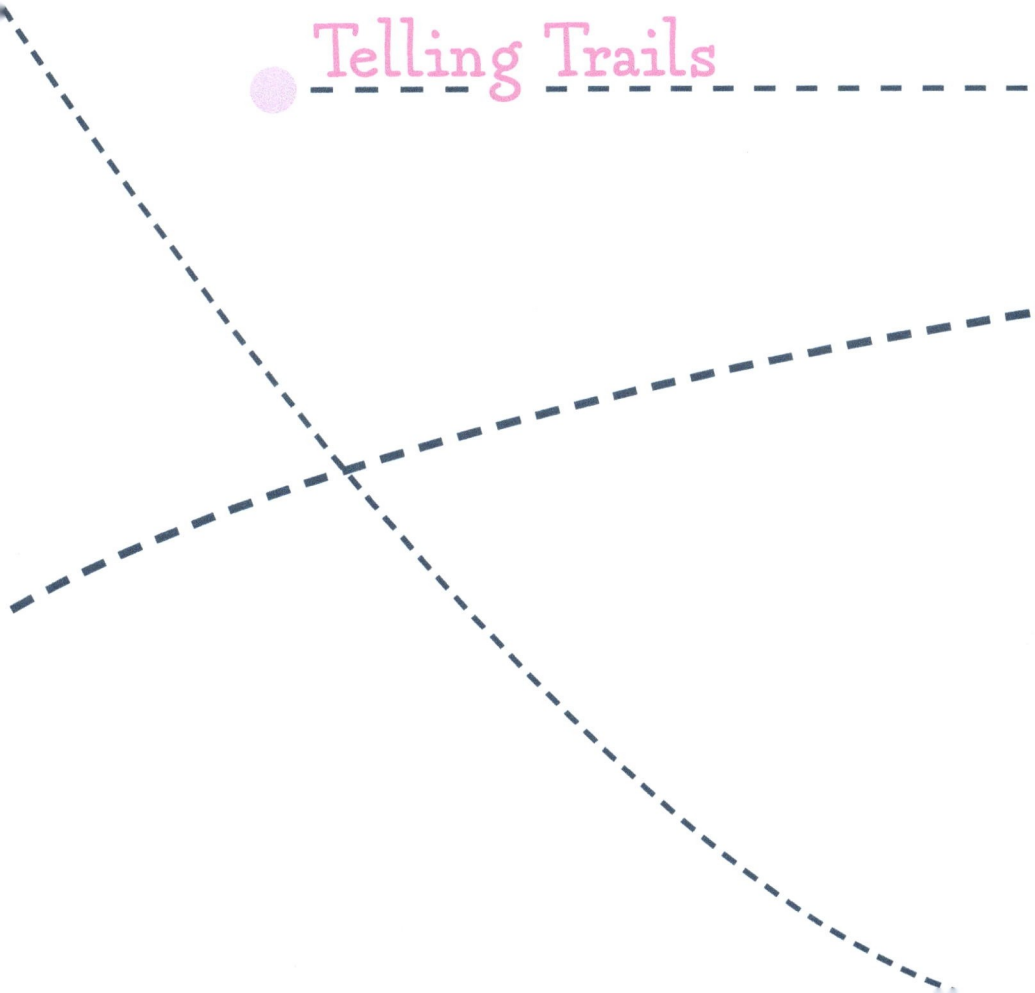

Your Story, Your Experiences, You!

In pictures, poetry and prose.

Iris Jackson

Cliffhanger PressWorks
Epigraph Books
Rhinebeck, NY

Hardcover ISBN 978-1-954744-30-1

Library of Congress Control Number 2021913645

Book design by Colin Rolfe

Photo credits:
Instagram:
@Philomena Photog
@Cakechick1218
@Keely E
www.keelyedwards.website/books

GlenArtistry@gmail.com GlenDatresArtWorks.Etsy.com

Star Wars: The Empire Strikes Back. Performance of Yoda, by Frank Oz. Directed by, Irvin Kirshner. Written by Lawrence Kasdan, Leigh Brackett, & George Lucas. Producers Gary Kurtz & George Lucas, 1980. "Game" image: Lucasfilm Ltd. The HASBRO, HASBRO GAMING, and MONOPOLY (1935. 2020) Hasbro, Pawtucket, RI, USA, HASBRO CANADA, LONGUEUIL, OC, CANADA J4G1G2.™ denote U.S. Trademarks
Gupta, Sanjay, Interview. Conducted by John LaPook, Jan 3, 2021, "*Keep Sharp: Build a Better Brain at Any Age*", Simon & Schuster.
Seuss, Dr. *Oh, the Thinks You Can Think!* Random House, 1975.
---*Oh, the Places You'll Go!* Random House, 1990.

Cliffhanger PressWorks
cliffhangerpressworks.com
Epigraph Books
22 East Market Street, Suite 304
Rhinebeck, NY 12572
(845) 876-4861
epigraphps.com
tellingtrails.org
tellingtrailstour@gmail.com

Dedication

To my friends, family, students and supporters…
Thank you so much for your unconditional love and collective wisdom, while I take this journey into a new world of books.

Some special photo inspirational dedications…
Thanks to:

T - for the "Red" and the joyful reading as well.

J - for loving times with "Java" , "Games" , "Dessert" and "Valentine"

C & A - for "real" book talks, music, dinners & amazing memories

P - for advice and motivational thoughts

NB - for clay cafe moments of clarity and sincere friendship

P.K. - networking, photos & long-lasting possibilities

PL - for special conversation, visits and inspirational dishes

J, J, L & T - for Wednesday, (sometimes Thursday & Friday) and next Week too

R - for "Kitten", new & loving memories.

Game Night Zoomers - for humorous and perpetual friendships

Dara & Monday Writers, B, C, M, R, & T - for feedback, supportive ears, & confidence boosters

C, C & J - for "Queen" co-workers and wonderful friends

V - for A-Z, "Bridge" to "Notes" with insightful, deserving, smart encouragement

M - from Childcraft to Publication and Beyond!

L.P.C. - for strength, courage and honesty to share

"We're not here for a long time, but for a Good Time"

Telling Trails is for that Kindergarten Gap Year. It's for dementia prevention and helpful for reluctant or emerging writers. It's for you to Be Creative. It's my version of journaling that is way less daunting. Whether in a drawing, in an idea, purpose or actual activity, a "Telling Trail" is for Fun!! Learn By Doing. The Best Learning Experiences Ever: where learning and insight sneak up on you. A "Telling Trail" prompts something in you. It moves you to do something. To do something New. It's all about DOING. As Yoda says... "Try not. Do, or do Not. There is no try." So DO Read on. Get up and Do your own "Telling Trail". And when the picture of what you experience outside, with your child, with your friend, or by yourself, spurs a thought within You, just write it down. You then have composed your own "Telling Trail"

I was prompted throughout the 2020 lockdown and work-from-home period, to DO as many "other" things that I could making the different places in my home seem like places to GO. Places I went. Places where positive things could be happening. Places to Do New things that I always or never thought I wanted to Do. To cook. (woah), To write.

To write a Book. So, I began and wrote and continued to write and observe and write. See things, listen to things, think about things, (WORK from home), Stress, and then finally Release from stress. Make Summer seem like summer. And continue to Want to write. To share, but somehow differently than in the social media way.

A Learning Way. A "Create" way. Not just a creative way - but a Way to Create. Do things that I was, and am becoming interested in. DO things that I wanted to do. (Within the confines of being mostly home - being "safe" from Covid) Do things that were valuable, worthwhile, made a difference. Do things that are FUN for Me. Writing that is meaningful. Meaningful to me. Fulfilling a personal goal. But, for it to really count (for me), and be meaningful - for me - would mean my writing could, would, should be meaningful to others. The best way I know to do that, is to make it a learning experience.

After a long career in education, I'm kinda hard-wired that way. Also, seems to serve me well in keeping me sane - instead of dwelling on the OMG, how bad was that. Am I worthy? Whining and complaining???? No way. I no longer Have Time NOR Make time for that. Rather, learning experiences make things meaningful to the collective "people" and/or on an Individual level. How does this have meaning for you?

So, it's not a judgement on what I'm writing - SOOOO different than how many social media things are "liked", evaluated, or commented on. Nope! This learning is for YOU. A self discovery. Your own personal thought process. Followed by, something You actually DO. Meaning, what you DO after - not, I like/join/click on someone else's idea, It's more than that. It's You moving forward and doing. Realize for you, maybe the idea comes first, maybe not. What's important in moving forward - is You doing Something. That is an action. Your action. Originated from YOU - Your own thought or feeling about something, now is manifesting in Doing. Your thoughts about what you felt because of it: and then You making a change, a move, directing an action - You, taking yourself from In your head, to making it happen.

EXAMPLE

| **I** | turtle, tree |

Turtle, turtle in that tree   hides where only I can see.
You can surely see it too   fun that we can share all new

This little poem came to me after taking a hike in a state park, where it was sunny, yet cold and snowy. One weekend day where a Mom and 2 children called out to me, "Look here! Do you see what's in this tree? Think you can find it? (I saw it.) Maybe you can find it too. You'll never guess what it is." I said, "Hi – I'll look and see what you mean, in that tree. Thanks!" So, had I Not acknowledged this cute family group, I might not have ever written this.

A little background on how that "Telling Trails" Writing came to be… Putting all these together for me came from all my activities from the past year and my desire to make my writing a positive learning experience for Me and for my "eventual" readers. Kicking off the idea was a short news story that some parents are choosing for their young children - to take a "Gap Year" before Kindergarten. Hmmmmm, well, Yes, I get that. All Home for school, is NOT the traditional Kindergarten. It's not the, oh so very needed, inter-personal contact of 5 year olds being together in a NEW fully functioning, setting, where they get to meet, play and learn with and from other children their own age. Live, In-Person Children who are not in their family, do not appear on TV, YouTube, Cartoons or Video Games. Actual living, breathing children who could, should, and will become their Peers. And with this present, live interaction, they could actually have the chance to become friends!! Real world Friends!!!! More than virtual, click an emoji like, press a button "poof" now you're my friend, While those friends have their place, (I suppose), These FRIENDS who you can see without the help of a camera, computer or screen, need to be met. They long to be met in person - (seen, touched, heard, chosen to play games with). And many more things yet undiscovered, by Kindergarteners.

DING - oh, a Learning experience here - Anyway, if this IN-Person learning and playing and gathering and friendship is NOT yet possible this year, I can totally understand why parents and even the children themselves, would choose to take a Gap Year until they could enjoy all the benefits of In-Person learning. DING - Idea... Could my writing be helpful in this way? I'm thinking that this may be possible. A Learning Experience. for the child, the parent, the parent and child. Learning individually and together. Hmmmm.... I'm liking this!!

Then additional articles / stories /research / books/ interviews discussing the fear of, research on, prevention of, loss of sleep type worry over Dementia. OMG, I forgot where I put my keys, am I in the initial stages of dementia? OOOoops, I forgot all about that appointment today.

This may of course be the fact that

a. Every day spent in or around home could be considered "Blursday"
b. You never learned how to use the calendar feature on your phone

And, really, the "dots" on the calendar feature on your phone, don't seem to have the urgency of writing it down on an actual paper calendar or planner.

Or, "that" discussion. You know, the one you had with your Mother. Or the one You are now having with your friend, or your own child. You know.. That guy, who was in That Movie. I'm sure Ya know. The one with the things that does all that stuff with the what-cha-ma-call-it. Look, anyone who has ever spoken to their Mother, Grandmother, Great-Grandmother, Auntie or even friend. (those people you used to see on a regular basis, yeah - them), You all know what I'm talking about. And you really only know how Close you are to the person who can't remember the Actor's Name, nor the specific Title of the movie they were starring in, when the person giving the "unbelievably ridiculous hints" on the name of the Actor = YOU, yes, you - Suddenly Know WHO they are talking about AND can even come up with their actual Name and the TItle of the Movie they were in. So, NO, this is Not dementia. In fact, these kind of stories are normal. No, in fact, These stories become "family stories" that you tell over and over again at Thanksgiving. (Oooops, well, maybe not in 2020. But hopefully soon, in some not-so-distant New Year, a Thanksgiving or holiday or just a dinner together in-person)

The fear and worry about dementia has occupied quite a lot of the band-width in people's minds and hopefully continues on in the medical research community. One such was an interview of Dr. Sanjay Gupta, by another doctor, Dr. John LaPook. The Book "Keep Sharp" by Sanjay Gupta, opens up the research on Cognitive Reserve and how to tap into it so that you can, in effect, Keep (yourself) Sharp. Dr. Gupta distilled the current research into basically doing activities that enlist the brain, the body, and your emotions. So, the suggestion was to take daily walks, with a friend, who you can speak to about your feelings/problems/emotions.

From my own current year's writings, hiking, thinking, being home, working from home, computer professional development courses, ZOOM, Google Meet, making videos, watching tv, reading, exercising, eating, cooking, baking, playing music - and _____ (fill in the blank _____ with your activities of 2020)

.... I've come up with the book: Telling Trails

Through this and future volumes, it is my intention to make this a positive learning experience for you. For you, your child, your parent(s), your friend - whomever you choose to share it with.

Start at your comfort level. Both the walking, the writing and the inspiration for the writing and walking. The start can be shared or individual, but either way personal for you. Find your comfort level. Your comfort level in walking and writing, Find your inspiration. It may be the person you choose to walk with. It may be just getting out. It may be making the time in your schedule, to get out and walk. It's all up to you. Then go for it. Walk and see what you see. Take pictures. *Take the Telling Trails templates at the back of the book,* and write what you see. Write what you hear. Write what you feel. Take a picture. Write the words that come to you. Words that came to your friend or your child. Maybe draw a picture instead. Or just doodle about what's in your head. (um, yes! Sometimes these things "may" rhyme. It's not necessary. It's not required. It can be plain, or one word, just the same) (Ooops, can't help it, it's an occupational hazard - or creative book (as referenced hereafter, just look. Haha!) Write one word to describe your picture. Then it may become more.

It just may trigger something in store...In the storage of your mind. That happened in a time that you may have been walking or talking. Or find that these things were just in your head. Somehow just now yearning just to be said. Or just to come out. So there is no doubt that you are uniquely YOU. No matter what you do.

And for the kids, it's just the same. Only you have to help them give it a name. And a time and a place, making room and some space. To learn what you know, so they can give it a go, while they're learning and earning more knowledge to grow into humans that can express themselves rightly and so.

AND, yes,,,, So, as I was saying...In the beginning, for you, find your comfort zone.

Get going. Walking, taking photos, doodling, drawing, writing. Assess where you are. Express your feelings. Tell someone, whether aloud or on paper. You may enjoy speaking or showing them later. Tell them your things, whenever, now, no reason, until one day, there may, be a way, or a time and a place, to speak face to face.

Writing could help you also avoid misunderstandings in that you thought, wrote, read and edited, before anything was said. You can be better understood when getting it out first and then expressing it to someone else. As stated before, children need instruction on how to do these things. The instruction can be from your Telling Trails. A fun way of spending time together and then when you write, you are "modeling" for your child. Then, if You do it, They can too. If they see you do it, then it's absorbed as important or something we all should do. Part of a routine. Tune in to the non-verbal cues and clues. Theirs and yours. Cultivate the "human side": together - Strong yet kind, fierce while observant. Listen with respect and respect will be returned to you. Then, when writing comes up as a school assignment, writing may not be as much of a scene. Instead, writing can be an activity they know and are familiar with, so an automatic response to pick up a pencil or pen, rather than pitching a fit. Or asking you to do it for them.

Telling Trails is a great way to apply what you know. The application of knowledge serves you as a functioning person, participating in society. Speaking these words with others, is *Worlds* better than just being a walking encyclopedia. (Oh,oops, sorry, Let me say it this way, that old fashioned big book that has information in alphabetical order). Or should I say, Telling Trail writing makes you a more complete person, rather than an awkwardly speaking human trivia game.

Telling Trails is beneficial in many phases of life. For your heart, soul and health. Try it, you'll see. Scribble it down, And then write back to me!!

Hint Words — to help jump start —

Inspiration can come from anywhere, you have to figure out how, when & where. Here's some things to help make your writing a habit. When you find one that works for you...
Just go out and Grab it!!

All good times to write, reflect & think - keep paper & pen, crayons, or recording devices handy to write and/or film your thoughts.

You may group them by first letter, or by time in the year, whatever works better.
Who knows, days of the week may work for you.
See what you like. See it all as You.

January, June, July	February	March
April, August	May	September
October	November	December

Monday	Tuesday	Wednesday	Thursday	Friday	Saturday	Sunday

Contents

This table of contents is unique to me....
It will be unique to you too, you will see;
I'm using the order each poem came to be....
You can do that too - or start with ABC;
If you so choose, you can rearrange these.....
to ABC order, if you please;
And let your young pal rearrange it for you....
See if they have a different order or two;
Maybe they know which way to go......
For finding what they want to show.

From the Beginning....number. 1
Letters for you. Go out and have fun!

I Turtle, Tree

Turtle, turtle in that tree hides where only I can see.
You can surely see it too fun that we can share all new

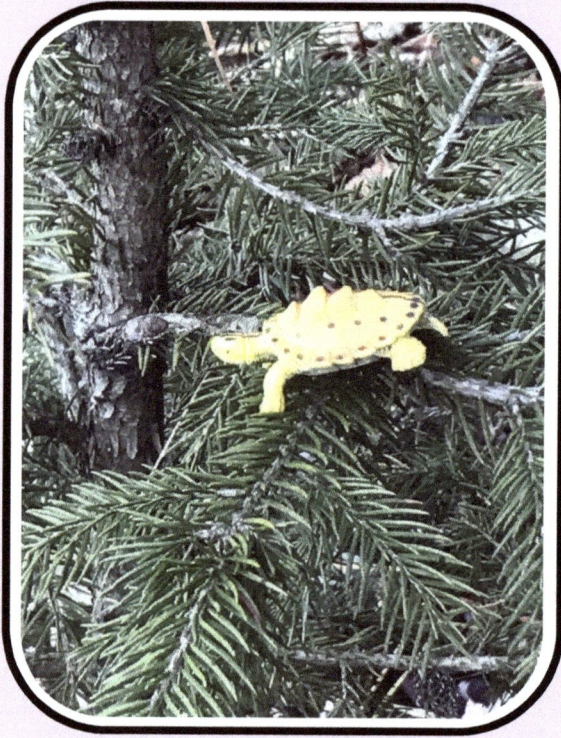

Do turtles live in trees? What do you think?
What else could be there? Draw it in ink.

T telling trail, turtle, tree, today, teacher, terrific, terrible, total

Today, today, it's Telling Trail time today .
What inspired you? Can you say?
Something you saw? Something you heard?
Maybe a cat, or a dog, or a bird.
Something you looked at? Something you said?
Or something that just popped into your head.
Write it, draw it, before you forget.
They'll point to new ones you haven't seen yet.

Now it's your turn

T is for _____

T _____

_____

_____

_____

_____

S

sun, shining, snow, slippery, silver, sky, scene, science, season, sunset, song

See the Sun. See the Tree. See it now? You and Me
See the shine on snowy branches. See it shine, Perfectly
See it high in the sky. See it together, You and I.
Saw it today, and what do you say?
You and I can see some more on another day!

And.... Here's some more. Once you get started....
Oh, it's hard to stop!

Seeing it with you makes all the seeing worth it!
On other days, you feel differently and may see and write
something else with the same letters you used before.
It's ok, that just shows there's so much more!
Sometimes we feel sad and it's ok - it's ok to feel that way.
When something happens or you just feel bad,
Just know with love, thought, and time -
 moving forward, will be a new mountain to climb.

Song *
Maybe Your favorite song. Or your child's, or your friend's to
sing-a-long.

S | statue, sun, snow

Now it's your turn

S is for _____

S _____

_____

_____

_____

_____

I icicles, icecream

How many "I" words did you find? In the picture & in the rhyme? I am, I like, I will, I know, I'll go

I learned that all about me is "I".
I am, I go, I do
All these Telling Trails with you
I soooo like what I see!
Because we made it special – You and Me!

INSPIRATION: *Pictures from Telling Trails*
Nature, friend, family, partner who walks with you.
Music – music of nature, music on device,
Music you hear in your head once or twice,
Music all around – if you just listen, listen for the sound!
Things you hear and see – see around you, on your device or maybe TV

I used to say that rhyming was the teacher's disease,
an occupational hazard, if you please.
But, to tell you the truth, I always liked it. Now more than in my youth.
Then I wasn't as sure about the things way down deep in my core.
SO much more now that I have experienced life –
with musical words galore!
Hooray for all this and now some of that.
That I finally felt I could share more of that, in a chat?
With you, and her, and he and they. With them and me
and more than just I can see.
I believe it's true, for me and for you,
that sharing experiences has great value –
Today for some and for others tomorrow,
never know who wants to borrow.
The New and the True – it's all up to you – what you will do.
With the true – and the true for you.
And while we are apart our words show the art.
Which for some ventures on, and others, a new start –
A new start for you, finding anew,
What things we can find in our minds, feet and heart.

I icicles. icecream, I

Now it's your turn

I is for _____

I_____

_____

_____

_____

_____

L little library, look, like, love, lunch, list, last, lovely, lots, live, life, lucky

This Little Library is named for somebody special.
A great lady/teacher/friend of the rest for,
The people who will come to borrow.
Not just today, but even more-so, tomorrow.
While she is gone from here, we'll remember and shed a tear.
The sorrow over the years, will be replaced
with each little face
that chooses to enter this new little space.
For this is Your own new Library,
in this bright special place.
Where You can read and talk thru what you've learned,
On Your very own Telling Trail that you've named and earned.

Lucky, lucky, lucky me, everyday I can see
Examples passing by and on TV, of all the pain and misery
That thankfully hasn't gotten me. Not In a physical health way,
but emotionally - every single day.
No way that they deserve this, nor I, no way.
But have to thank G-d everyday
And my parents for having me be born at the right time,
And circumstances, putting me in the right place.
Or "signs" leading me toward new things, at a slower pace.
Slower since at home, on the computer,
Zooming, thinking, writing and such
Meeting, thinking, writing so much.
Taking the time to sit back and see, just how fortunately lucky,
I am to be me.

L letters, little library, Lady Liberty

My Room
My Home Address

September 2020

Dear School,
I'm writing to you since I don't see you much. I miss you and all my friends, oh so much. Even though I have a desk and a chair, it's not the same as really being there. So soon, I hope, I'll get to be and hear and see, All of you and everyone else too. The way it used to be.

Sincerely,
Student Soliloquy

Now it's your turn

L is for _____

L_____

_____

_____

_____

_____

_____

W walking, whistle, walking, wonder, wake, wish, well, water, wonderful, woke, whisper, welcome

Combination Letters - to compose more complex Telling Trail Writings.

S W storytelling, walking (Telling Trails)

Wonderful time, wonderful goal, wonderful to get out and stroll
Wonderful way to make the story of my day.
Of my day, of your day, how we work and how we play.
Seeing, hearing, talking, going
Feelings from inside and the feel of wind blowing
Caring, Sharing, composing & daring.
Our Telling Trail is for getting up and out to find a way to DO.
Your Telling Trails can be that way too.
Indoors to start, when it's too cold, or too private within your heart.
But moving it along and out, whether you want to whisper or shout.
Moving it outside will up your game
with a sense of pride that You did it! All the same.
In words did you confide. You wrote.
You got out, and saw and felt and spoke.
Spoke for yourself, spoke to your friend,
one who will support you till the end.
Spoke with wonder, spoke with thought, spoke with dreams and
wishes of what the experience brought.
Spoke to get outside - to move, to see, to hear to think,
Spoke with a friend, who with only a wink,
Will share in your journey now and forever,
See here, see now, Telling Trails - a time to treasure!

Now it's your turn

W is for _____

W_____

_____

_____

_____

_____

_____

Telling Trails

Combination Letters

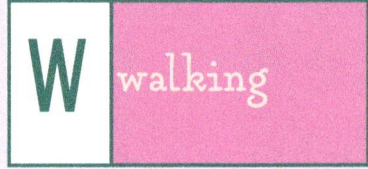

S storytelling   **W** walking

What's your favorite story?_____
_____

Where would you like to walk?_____
_____

Now it's your turn

S is for _____

W is for _____

S W_____
_____
_____
_____
_____

H	happy, healthy, heart, hope, help, helpful, hair, hunt, hole, hurt, history, holiday, hollow, huge, happy tears
F	flower, friend, Fall, forever, forgive, forget, forward, first, fable, flute, follow, family, fruit, feather, feelings
G	game, gift, girl, grow, growth, garage, glow, glorious, gloves, glory, glue, girly, glass, glassy, groovy

H, F, G -- Happy with Flowers! Happy playing a Game!
Happy things to do with you.
Each one makes me happy, all the same.
You know it, you know it's true - even if I don't always tell you.
You know by my smile. You know by my style
Of walking, or singing a song everyday.
You know how I love you. That's how we play.
You know I'm just so proud. Though I'd better not always say it aloud.
I know it gets too much. But, happy when cooking some very
yummy stuff.
Fun that we've had, even though when you're mad
The funny helps move that mad or sad to glad.
So glad we can spend this time together.
You and me kid, makes it all better.

G | game, girl, grow

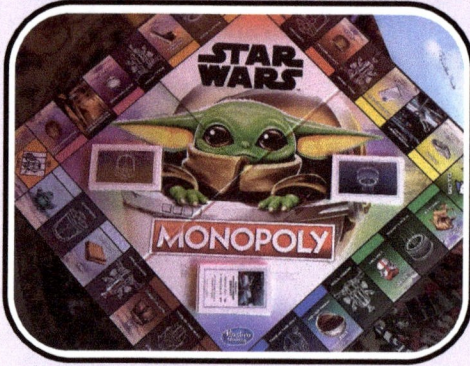

Now it's your turn

G is for _____

G_____

_____

_____

_____

_____

_____

H humorous, happy, healthy, hello

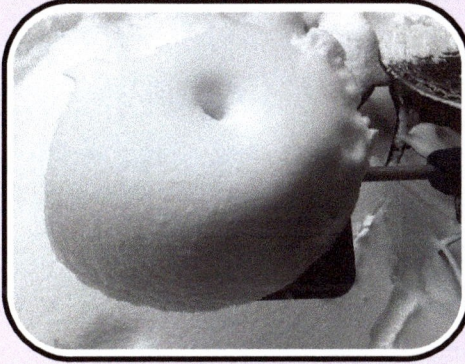

Hey, look.
It's a "snownut"!!

Now it's your turn

H is for _____

H_____

_____

_____

_____

_____

_____

F | flowers. friend, family

Now it's your turn

F is for _____

F_____

_____

_____

_____

_____

@ philomenaphotog

@ philomenaphotog

Your favorite flower

C cake, clouds, children

So proud of our kids! In everything they did.
How they learned, how they earned,
how they struggled through and
had a meeting of the minds with you.
So, proud of them all, no matter how big or small.
All this learning, so integral to their lives, one and ALL.

Or have fun with words that you especially like..

C - Choose
H - How your
I - Inventive
L - Likes and looks
D - Dawn on you,
R - Right now
E - Ending the day and entering
N - Nighttime dreams

@cakechick1217

C   clouds, children, cookies

Now it's your turn

C is for _____

C _____

_____

_____

_____

_____

_____

B bakery, book, bridge

So inviting - from sign to storefront - what do you think?
Shall we go in for lunch? - or maybe a drink?
Or just a coffee to check it out.
If coffee's good, there is NO Doubt.
A new spot to stop for liquid delight -
 gotta get that coffee, especially if it's right.
Let's check it out. What do you think?
Or more than a drink. Oh what do you think?
Shall we stop and go inside? Gotta make it worth the ride.
To shop and support those little places -
That could become our new happy spaces
Meeting new friends - same smiles on their faces
For the things that They bought from that place new to you,
Can also provide for the owners, and city, it's true.
Loving the journey, even though not too far.
We can get there on foot, no need for the car.
Will you be my new place for coffee and such?
Can't know till we go and find this new magic touch.
Gotta be worth the calories you know,
So get out and go, and then you will show
All your friends who like coffee, local goodies and such
All the places and spaces we are missing so much.

B — bridge, book, bakery

Now it's your turn

B is for _____

B_____

_____

_____

_____

_____

O order, other, otter, outside

A,B, C	1,2,3	ROYGBIV	C,D,E,F,G,A,B,C
	...in the court	"Yes, I'd like fries with that"	

Orders

These are some orders, yes indeed.
Some that you've made, some that you need.
Some you remember, some done each day
All pretty necessary in so many ways.
Although somewhat hard when washing your clothes
Or folding or putting them away, In time, I suppose.
Just think how it helps on the days you wake late
Or making a date or baking a cake.
The order does help and lets us remember
 The many things to your phone you surrendered.
So when they pop up, now and again
Remember too, when time was your friend.

O order, old, oak, opportunity

@PhilomenaPhotog

Now it's your turn

O is for _____

O _____

_____

_____

_____

_____

P pink, photo, pheasant, people, places, planet

Oh the places you'll go, or the Thinks you can think.
Said an old friend of mine, with a smile and a wink.
He's been my friend, forever and a day
He comes with me anywhere I go, some say.
Always liked rhyming, yes it's true.
Whether red or yellow, or green or blue
Even when red leaves me so frustrated and mad,
Or if I was blue, melancholy or sad
Or yellowish happy like a sunny day, I think
The green's calm and mellow - for me, that is pink.
So pink, starts with "P", this letter you see -
Unusual to wear on a hike after lunch Some people might stare
But where I did go, surely noone was there.
'Cept a man and his dog, looking for pheasant out there.
A surprise - don't you think to the girl wearing pink
The man and his dog found some mud and some ice
and a girl dressed in pink, who seemed very nice.
To share a moment to talk on this walk
'bout pheasants out there, that never were caught.
So, never you mind, and don't try to think
Of the reason they met this girl wearing pink.
Go out and explore the wide world, if you dare
The wide world outside and the one that's in there.
In there where you think of the girl dressed in pink
and the man and the dog near the ice, mud and fog.
What happens with them, right now, cannot say
Those thoughts I'll think up on some other sunny day.
That means your adventure's just beginning you see
Adventures you take with your friend and me.
Adventures you'll have, oh yes, have a ball
Trips in your mind that make sense of it all.

Write them all down - write them now, write them clear.
Write quickly and then, again. You have nothing to fear.
Read it over some time, some time when you think.
You'd like to know more 'bout the girl dressed in pink.

P | pink, power, please, paper

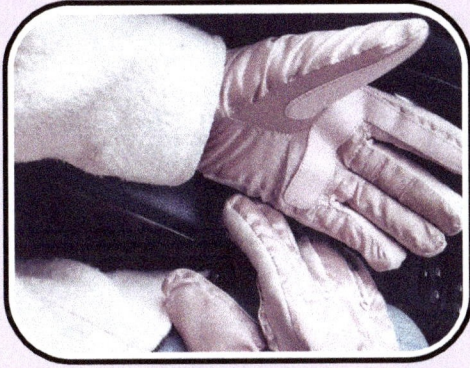

Now it's your turn

P is for _____

P_____

_____

_____

_____

_____

_____

M meet, man, mistake, mystery

You never really know who you're going to meet
In your neighborhood or on a far away street
Not that it was in your plan, to stand in line behind that man
That Man who heard your mistake
Over at that Post Office table - with the wrong address label.
So time to get back in line
when the label's all fixed and now all is fine.
You never know, as I said before, if you're 2, 3 or 4
But That Man realized it, and he knew the score
and waved me on by so I could be in front once more
He said that's how it should be 'cause I was there before he
And even with a mask you could see,
him smiling in the mask toward me.
So I thanked him and said what a kind thing to do
Keeping others in mind so pleasant and true.
As I mailed my package, I told the clerk
how kind the Man was to me
But it's no wonder as they are just as kind to me while they work.
So all here could smile, in knowing that kind people are found
Wherever you're going, in and around any town.

M mountain, man, meet

Now it's your turn

M is for _____

M_____

_____

_____

_____

_____

E enjoy, eggs, emotion

Enjoy the moments. Enjoy the time.
The thought, the emotion of things made right by rhyme.
These conversational walks, sharing seconds to talk
May or may never come again,
So cherish each day, over and over again.
Because it's always needed to cherish, honor and love
Those close to you - very near - so sincere - in your heart or above
Meaningful friends and family and those yet to meet.
What does it all mean?
What it means to you. To do, the whole day through
So tell those you love how much they all mean
Vocally, yes - sometimes better to address
On a page, for you now, or at another age
Just WRITE - say it loud
Just Write - say it proud
Just write for you and then, who knows who? Maybe a crowd?
Either way, in the alone times, those searching can find,
value in your very own rhymes
But then, later on, in the square
Can find peace in the words that you're willing to share.

E — eggs, enjoy, emotion, energy

Now it's your turn

E is for _____

E_____

_____

_____

_____

_____

A aspire, ambition, Amanda

Aspire you here, aspire to be,
so elegant and talented as Amanda - Laureate of Poetry.
One so young, so bold, so sincere,
All who would stand and cheer - Here, Here!
Here, here to her prose, Here, here to sway foes.
Here, here to all mothers, & fathers & beaus.

Amazed and excited by her presence & words.
Stood this teacher, mamma, and all watching who heard,
From the Capitol Steps and World Stage,
an Inaugural Poem for a brand new age.
From the age of one, who was so young.
Only young of years, but who moved elders to tears
Through Joy and pride in understanding all sides
Of the majesty of the moment, we all beam with pride.
Through verbs of simplicity, The hope, shall we Go
Forward with felicity, each from our row.
With the need for us all, through our collective faith,
Moving folks forward... forward from any race.
With new executive leaders, who help us plant seeds with grace.
To grow our Democracy with a mighty foundation
To share, one and all, with the people of our Nation.

The bridges we build, between the right, left and between.
We work hard for it now as it's rarely recently been seen.
In Action, individually and together we move,
To make and show and support and prove,
All things of promise, we pledge to listen and learn,
And strive to participate towards new friendships we earn.

With new Leaders of Service - we all share with pride.
A Woman of Color - South Asian and Black
and a Long standing Statesman with Love and experience at
his back

With a stroke of a pen, here we all go...
Into our new future - with family, friends and foe.
To fight for what's right and what's good and what's strong.
That, for us all, to help carry on
The traditions we seek, the traditions we share,
Traditions from all of us, here, there, and where.
That's what makes our Union so great,
Great together, from state to state.
To show what we know, and share how we care
About hopes and dreams becoming reality in our square.
The square when we started, the square that we sought,
To be, you can see, to be planned before, to be NOW, 123.
To be just a part of this country at work and at leisure,
No matter the height or the slight bit of measure,
We all count in this life, this life just the same
With all here together, under one sacred name,
OUR Country, our people, our old and young together
Share health, wealth and happiness and moments to treasure.

Oh what Telling Trails you could have in this lovely chair swing.
Just so beautiful, you could write Anything!

_____

_____

_____

_____

A | art, alone, ambition, aspire

GlenArtistry@gmail.com

Now it's your turn

A is for _____

A_____

_____

_____

_____

_____

_____

N notes, nature, nuts, nobody, never, notice

Did you ever notice the beauty in nature?
Did you ever notice that tree?
Did you ever notice when you're smiling, you're free?
Did you notice how big or how small? Or how straight or how curvy?
     Or my thrill when you call?
Did you notice the top or the bottom or side?
Or the corner I take, when you run and hide?
Did you notice the sun in the sky when it shines?
Or the rain when it falls? Or our dog when she whines?
Did you notice the route we took today,
was a little bit different, but you still knew the way.
Did you notice what was new?
I thought you did – how super for you!!
Did you notice I noticed and I told you too?
     That you're growing up, now what shall we do?

N notes, nature, notice, new

I wonder how the Notes sound on this Veena? A South Indian instrument similar to the sitar. Looks so cool, in the museum case. Oh so close…. Yet so far.

Now it's your turn

N is for _____

\
\
\
\
\
\

N_____

_____

_____

_____

_____

_____

Q queen, quartet, quest, quality, question

This is the quest - you and I - the Best
For others, maybe a test - what to do with the rest?
Quality, quality, quality - they say.
Gotta be quality.
Who are you to say you've got quality?
What makes you think you can do this?
Why do you think you have something to say?
Something to share?
Questions, questions, questions? Questions everywhere.
That's all good though. There's more out there,
More to think about. More to share.
And, isn't that the key?
Why, yes, yes it IS! You see...
Here's what you've got. You've got a lot.
A lot to say, each and every day.
Whether anyone is there to hear it live.... Who's to say?!
So write it down. Write it down. Write it down!
If you can see it, you can say it. To someone in-person, or
someone on a page. That's YOU on that page -
YOU - are someone - at any age.
So go do it. See it, Say it. Write it today.

Q queen, quiet, quest

Now it's your turn

Q is for _____

Q _____

_____

_____

_____

_____

J java, juice, Julie

Java, java, java jewel
My java every morning, my Java morning tool
Used to be at noon and evening too
However, much better in the morning for you.
Local roaster - I love to find
Local businesses - The best Kind
Kind as they are, sweet as can be
Close to my heart, my morning Coffee!

My favorite drink

J | java, joy, jubilee, juice

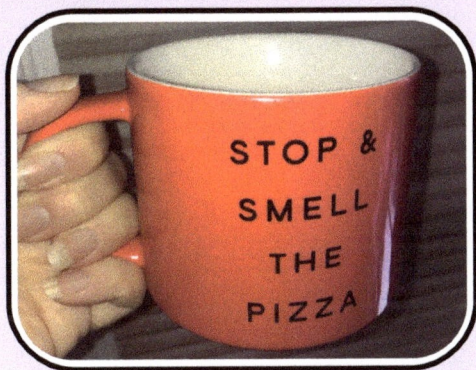

Now it's your turn

J is for _____

J_____

_____

_____

_____

_____

_____

K kitchen, kits, kite

So, Hello - Hello there - My Kitchen
Yes, you are my kitchen, My Kitchen
May I introduce or shall I say... Re-introduce myself to you.
You and I are now going to become Re-aquainted with each other.
Re-aquainted since I am going to be home.
Home... Lots more
Home - you and me - and everyone here
will expect a little bit more
So may I make a deal with you?
Yes, a deal - for you and I to try.
Meaning - Actually DO!
Do more cooking - Cooking?, Yes, Cooking!
You? No, ME - Yes, YOU, Couldn't be, then who???
SO Stop kidding around - You are always out on the town.
Very little time for me.
No pots and pans "sound". Really? You're gonna see Me?
See Me. I'm no longer out and about, nor free
Free from dirt and grease and burnt,
Well no - Didn't say that - Mistakes?
More than appearances, will it take.
For Me to become a chef of course,
Cooking, baking, cleaning of all sorts,
May I please, I beg of you -
Don't laugh too hard because - when I'm through,
I'll be back again,
with some other culinary invention for them.
Some created from a book, I promise some - Don't even look,
Don't look now, just show me how
To make THIS meal - no Big Deal. (haha)
Fake it till you make it?? Really, with food?? Oh my
Nah!! Make a tester batch - You taste it first, then make it better from scratch.
From scratch you say? Getting better every day.
Holy Gee - this is Me?
Ingredients, mixing bowls, spices and recipes.
Woah - who would have thought?
Who thought this of Me?
Least of all -- yours truly, you see?
But this is fun. This is it. This is ME!
Thank you supermarket, green grocer, friends and family
So glad we did it! My kitchen and Me.
MY kitchen and Me. Can be friends forever.
Thank you my Kitchen!! And...More Power to ME!

K kitten, kitchen, kite, kind

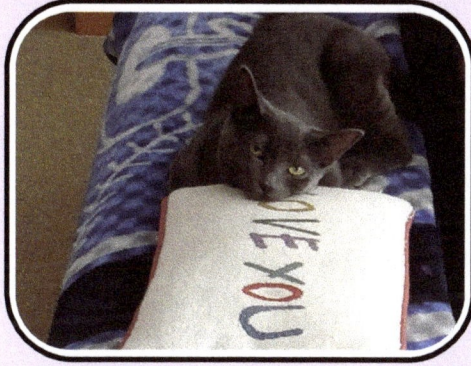

Now it's your turn

K is for _____

K_____

_____

_____

_____

_____

Z zoo, zip, zigzag, zipper

The ZOO!!
I so very missed seeing animals from far and wide
The Lions in their pride stirs a feeling of awe - I just can't hide
Oh to Zip on a plane to maybe see for myself
Instead of only my well-loved toy on my shelf.
Or maybe check these amazing animals on-line
And decide where I'll go to see, when I get time.
Time and days and months seems so crazy
No, no, no - it's NOT that I'm lazy.
It's just that one day blends into another.
Just like lunch and dinner and school, all done with my Mother.
Not that I mind her, I quite love her a lot.
It's just hard in the same place, all the time.
To give it All you've got - like it or not.
But like it or not, that's what we must do.
If we ever hope to travel, on a train or a plane, or even to the zoo.

Z zoo, zip, zither

I so love the zoo!
As a child, seeing all the animals, right in front of me.
Ones that I could have only seen in a book, or on TV
Or on a special trip to somewhere nature related.
Can't say how much I've anticipated,
Being able to go again, with a friend
Or another child to show the wonders of the world we know,
and worlds we don't yet
And all those we hope to save, and never forget.

Now it's your turn

Z is for _____

Z _____

_____

_____

_____

_____

Y you, yellow, yesterday

You are always you, no matter what you say or what you do.
You are big and bold and brave.
You are my friend, my hope, my hero, my sage.
You see the moon and the stars and never ask why.
Only, "Can I see them myself?", So it's my job to help you to try.
You are my pride, my joy, my life.
I see more each day. I'm so lucky, this now is My life,
We're living in the part of history people write about.
We will remember this.
You will remember this.
They will remember this.
WOW! All of this.

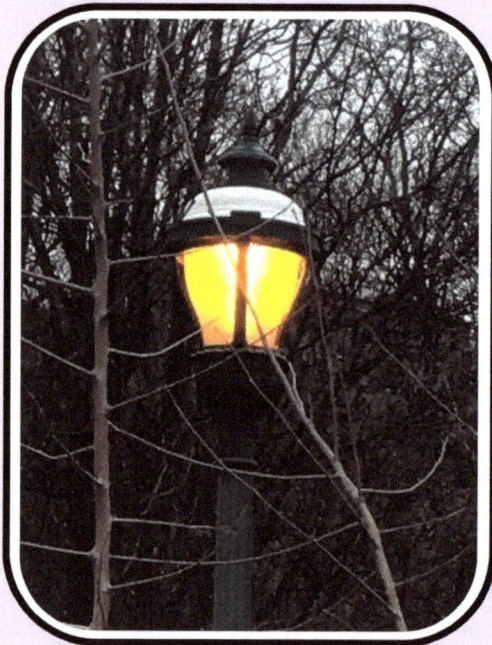

Y yellow, yesterday, yes

@PhilomenaPhotog

Now it's your turn

Y is for _____

Y_____

_____

_____

_____

_____

X   x-ray, xylophone

Ok, now X is a letter that's got some things that define.
Things you really need, some of the time.
OK, here it is: x-ray.
Yup, you need these, for your teeth, your leg if you fell and it hurts
Or sometimes for things that are even worse.
Like many of the reasons we are home and not around and about.
On computers for school or work –
TOO MUCH TIME HERE – you shout.
So, let's X-ray the situation, and see if we can find a better station.
At least for the letter "X" which for now, is My vocation.
For me, X is special for xylophones – not only for their lovely tones,
But the joy they bring to all who try,
to find music and reach for the sky.
X is just like that, with some help from some other letters.
Like "E" that helps make it eXtrordinary.
X is eXcellent when you eXplore
all the fantastic things the world has in store
For you as you grow, And for me, who supposedly knows
All the things that Could be,
when we do our Telling Trails – Just you and me.

X xray, xylophone, eXtra, eXcellent, eXciting

Yeah!   Hooray!!   Woo Hoo!!!   Go For It!!!!
Exciting words. Exciting phrases.
   Exciting things & Exciting places.
Soon, oh soon, we hope to go,
   Keep in mind and Remember though...
It's not how far, but how you feel...
   A very near thing, can be a very exciting, big deal!!

Now it's your turn

X is for _____

X _____

_____

_____

_____

_____

_____

D dream, day, decision, doctor, dilemma, delicious, drive

Dream. Dream? Dream! Do you dream? Do you know?
Did you dream? Tell me so.
Really, truly, honestly, I don't know.
What would they show? That I'm crazy? This doesn't go...with that!
How could you dream up a flying cat?
Or water, or a train??? Hmmm.. All crazy, crazy, Insane.
Could be a dilemma or delicious!
Or that you need a doctor - So don't repeat this!
Or maybe just a time to download your brain,
Get restorative sleep so you don't go insane.

Sleep well, dream if you can, or if you must.
Why not get the best out of life?
Whether awake or asleep, no need for strife.
Live your life as you live your dream.
Make it, Take it and swim down the stream.
To wherever it takes you. Wherever the stakes you claim and work up to.
Building your life with courage and drive,
Using the tools that make you YOURSELF and greatly Alive.
Take these dreams and make them your life,
Plan to take crazy and make it your own.
Turn it into useful and and something you've grown
Into joy and spirit and make it complete
So others can see it and hear it and speak.
How crazy became wonder, and knowledge and fun.
And that spreads to others, but before you are done
It grows like a weed, showing passion indeed
And grace and speed as it grows evermore
 from your dream, to your desk, to construction, then store.
Gaining speed and what's more,
it's use inspires others to dream while they snore
Even during the day, when your work could be play
Taking your dream from a deep place inside
To a forum that fills you with pride
Of a job well done. Well done, now in the sun.
The sun of a new day, where others can play
And dream of a way- where they rise and say..
Now it's my turn, and I'll seize the day.

D | dessert, dog, draw, dream

@cakechick1217

Now it's your turn

D is for _____

D _____

_____

_____

_____

_____

V vote, view, visionary, vibrant, visit, victory, vegetable

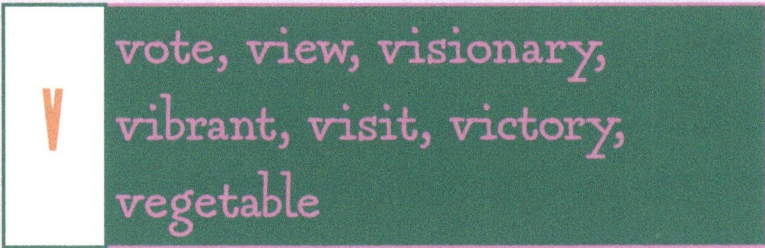

Answered my Ask! WOAH – my Vote, my elected rep.,
answered my email. Now here's the task
That's a tale for today.
They responded to me, the internet channel way.
Am I up to the task? Of putting the right words, behind the Ask.
Will they really listen? Will they care?
Only one way to know. Join the Zoom call and Share.

What would you vote for?

Where would you visit?

V valentine, vision, vote, vegetable

Now it's your turn

V is for _____

V _____

_____

_____

_____

_____

_____

| R | "R" (are) rhyme, rhythm |
| U | "U" (you), understood, use, ultimate |

R - Rhyme - that's what I seem to be doing, a lot of the time.

R U aware of the way that you speak?
On the phone, I mean text, or on paper, or with a tweet?
RU to realize what shortcuts you take
May have effects on the sense that you make?
Some "get it" as matter-of-fact,
some mistake the whole thing and get you off track.
Not good with a co-worker nor a friend
Wrong meanings could spark the beginning of the end.
Or worse with a boss, whose power could mean
The end of your work at this place, and what's worse
The next place who "heard" it, oh my, what a curse.
So here's my advice for the moments past and present,
Write it down and read it before you go send it.
Read it and edit and see what's really meant.
Before it goes into cyber space to befall
Any who read it, that's IT and that's ALL.
And for those who prefer actual pen and paper,
GO ahead and write on, if that is your nature.
And your young friends who come on Telling Trails with you,
Take this learning to heart and save through and through
As YOU helped them be, Be all that they could.

R   U

When sharing your life on this street, in the wood.
Of the places you live in and the places you'll go
When walking together, sharing time, place and mo'
All the memories you'll have when you write it all down.
Write it all down, about you, your friend and your town.
All the sights and the smells and the thoughts and the sound.
Share it now, share it later, all these moments to savour
When you're away, far or near,
Where only you can hear, without any fear
Your thoughts and memories of time so dear
With your Mom, your child, your friend – with a slight little tear
Of Telling Trails and time to compose your own book
And the Wonder of life, and the time that you took.

R red, ready, "R" (are)

Now it's your turn

R is for _____

R_____

_____

_____

_____

_____

_____

U underneath, use, ultimate, "U" (you)

Now it's your turn

U is for _____

U_____

_____

_____

_____

_____

_____

So, now it's Your Turn! (As I've said on every accompanying page throughout the book). While the book was written for you to have the opportunity throughout the process, it continues to be your turn. You had, and still have permission, the right, the inspiration, the hope, the dream, the learning experience, the friendship experience, the Parent/Child experience or any formation of all of the above. All of these are expressly YOURS to use and enjoy as you wish.

It is my sincere hope that you have gained something for yourself by reading and taking your own Telling Trails. Enjoy the activities, routines and feelings that walking, meeting together, and new adventures bring, and then writing it down to express it all. Telling Trails helps take you where your mind and body, meet friendship, nature, and activity. The ideas spurred on by the activity can be shared by writing words or phrases on each individual page, drawing what you see and hear, speaking about your thoughts and feelings. Each of these activities makes the experiences "real" and a memory without necessarily a fancy title (Reflections on....

Journal of…), without a deadline or spell-check.

This is YOURS to have and to hold,
to share, if you are so bold,
To honor and cherish, like your friend or your child,
Or just something beautiful that lasts for a while.
And if you wish, or so desire,
To take your journey higher and higher
The choice is yours to share but only if you dare.
Share when it's right for you, day or night.
These may become your songs of joy, of fear,
of memories far or oh so near.
Get out there and do it and you will see
Your thoughts and words bring learning experiences
or those yet to be.

As is the point... Your Telling Trails are moving, movable, adaptable to your mood.

So is this book Really for Me?
Oh yes, because it IS YOU, you see?

As the thought came to me, and as will come to you...
This Book IS, really is, just for You!!!

It is totally customizable -
It's on your time, in your place,
Alone or with whomever you choose to be,
in the same or another place.
At this time or later on - Always at Your own pace.
Using your own thoughts, legs, arms and face.
Just you and what you want, need or choose to give.
This is for YOU and how you are, or would like to live.

No one is there to force this on-line,
or IG or Snap or any of that kind.
It's You and what you want, in your own time.
Paper and pencil are just fine.
Draw or shoot photos too, that's part of the rhyme

scheme that works for you,
and maybe your child or your Grandma or friend too
No assembly required, only this guide, if you take it for the ride.
Noone says it has to have tech
But in learning and doing new things? Ah, what the heck?!
Go there too, if you choose. Unless you think you have some-
thing to lose.
Although, what would you lose? The fear of the unknown?
Depends on the type of learning you choose.
It's all up to you. Whatever you see, or feel or write or draw.
Your own personal habit, routine, or daily law.
It's all here for you. It always was, It's now shaped in a book.
A Story of You, A new one, if you're willing to look.
SO YES, this IS for you. For you alone,
for you and how you're willing to share.
It will be here for you, anytime, anywhere.
Just get up and go. See and do.
It's all out there, just waiting for you!

From me - to you, the tool!

The Template that I used and created for you.
One to take, or draw on and write
Right after your Telling Trail, or later on that night.
One you can use to tell your tale,
And share with others, or read privately without fail.

And also from someone more learned than I…
Who feels the same way,
Your turn, Oh my!

"If you want to teach people a new way of thinking,
don't bother trying to teach them,
Instead give them a tool, the use of which will lead to
new ways of teaching" - Buckminster Fuller

"For the actions you take can fulfill your own dreams,
and inspire some others who would dare, it seems
to make theirs come true on their own Telling Trials
In their time, in their space, in their own special place,
Where they talk as they walk, taking care as they share."
- Iris Jackson

To My Dear Friend,

While I am so sad not to share this with you in person, I am so grateful to honor you with my book that I hope is worthy of your name - POWERS - I have always felt that while you kept this as your middle name, that it is at your core that you Are "Powers". Powers in thought, and mind and body and spirit -

In friendship, in love, in character and confidence. You exemplify what it is to be a friend - a teacher - a leader - a sister in sustaining what is good and right with the world, along with the POWERS to move it all forward.

Your friends, your family, and all of the thousands of students in the city and on the east coast who were fortunate enough to have benefitted from being in your presence will be able to move it all forward because of you. With a crumb of your courage, an ability to facilitate experiential knowledge, and the strength to lead in whatever challenges could arise, we will be able to move forward.

I am so fortunate to have shared in a small yet mighty piece of each of your lives academic, public and private - and hope that my words, and the words of those who choose to take a Telling Trail of their own, discover the extraordinary pieces of strength in themselves, as you have shown me. Love to you LPC in your next journey!

- So in my own Telling Trails way....

Seeing it with you makes all the seeing worth it!
...Just know with love, thought, and time –
moving forward, will be a new mountain to climb.

LPC - had said and lived by....

"We're not here for a long time,
We're here for a good time!"

Author Bio

Iris Jackson's debut publication is one born out of many years of experience in the field of education. Writer, educator, & musician, Ms. Jackson is the author of "Telling Trails", a must-have for those who want to travel and explore the art within themselves. Through the joy of sharing poetry & prose, drawings & photography, bring your binoculars and your companions to places you may have never explored in a simply enjoyable way.

From the Hudson Valley, through the East Coast and beyond, you can share your Telling Trails in a growing community of storytellers at Cliffhangerpressworks.com or at Tellingtrails.org

TellingTrailsTour@gmail.com

Telling Trails Template

Now it's your turn...

_____ (letter)

This letter is for _____

Tell about your picture and your letter.

_____

_____

_____

_____

_____

_____

Telling Trails Take-a-Long Template

Telling Trails

Letter _____

Words _____

_____

Picture / Writing

Telling Trails

Letter _____

Words _____

_____

Picture / Writing

Telling Trails Take-a-Long Template

Telling Trails

Letter _____

Words _____

_____

Picture / Writing

Telling Trails

Letter _____

Words _____

_____

Picture / Writing

Telling Trails Template

Now it's your turn...

A is for ___Author, and all that I can be too!___

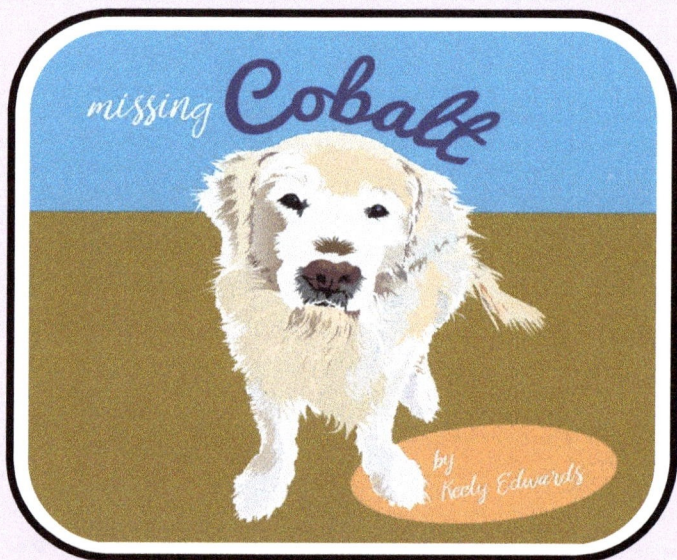

missing **Cobalt**

by Keely Edwards

Keely E, IG, www.keelyedwards.website

Tell about this picture and becoming an author

_____
_____
_____
_____
_____
_____
_____

www.ingramcontent.com/pod-product-compliance
Lightning Source LLC
Chambersburg PA
CBHW040418110426

42813CB00013B/2689